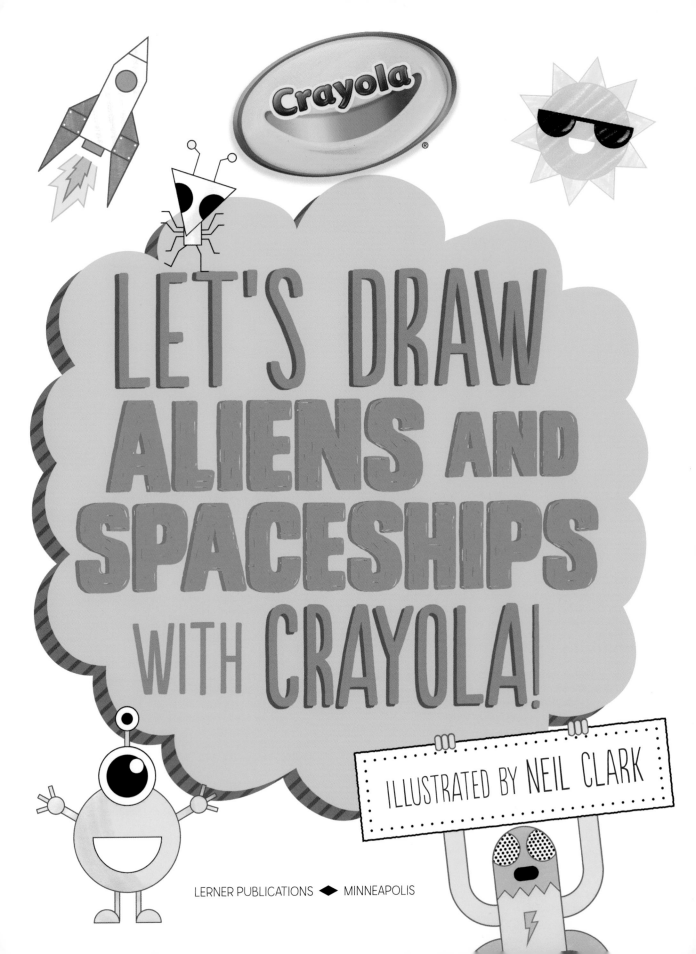

LET'S DRAW ALIENS AND SPACESHIPS WITH CRAYOLA!

ILLUSTRATED BY NEIL CLARK

LERNER PUBLICATIONS ◆ MINNEAPOLIS

© 2018 Crayola, Easton, PA 18044-0431. Crayola Oval Logo, Crayola, Serpentine Design, Shadow, Timberwolf, Banana Mania, Inchworm, Outer Space, Vivid Violet, Pink Flamingo, and Pink Sherbert are registered trademarks of Crayola used under license.

Official Licensed Product
Lerner Publications Company
A division of Lerner Publishing Group, Inc.
241 First Avenue North
Minneapolis, MN 55401 USA

For reading levels and more information, look up this title at www.lernerbooks.com.

Main body text set in Billy Infant Regular 24/30.
Typeface provided by SparkyType.

Library of Congress Cataloging-in-Publication Data

Names: Clark, Neil, 1981 June 4- illustrator.
Title: Let's draw aliens and spaceships with Crayola! / illustrated by Neil Clark.
Description: Minneapolis : Lerner Publications, 2019. | Series: Let's draw with Crayola! | Audience: Ages 4–9. | Audience: K to Grade 3.
Identifiers: LCCN 2018003932 (print) | LCCN 2018016774 (ebook) | ISBN 9781541512559 (eb pdf) | ISBN 9781541511033 (lb : alk. paper)
Subjects: LCSH: Outer space—In art—Juvenile literature. | Extraterrestrial beings in art—Juvenile literature. | Drawing—Technique—Juvenile literature.
Classification: LCC NC825.09 (ebook) | LCC NC825.09 L48 2019 (print) | DDC 743/.8—dc23

LC record available at https://lccn.loc.gov/2018003932

Manufactured in the United States of America
1-43987-34001-8/13/2018

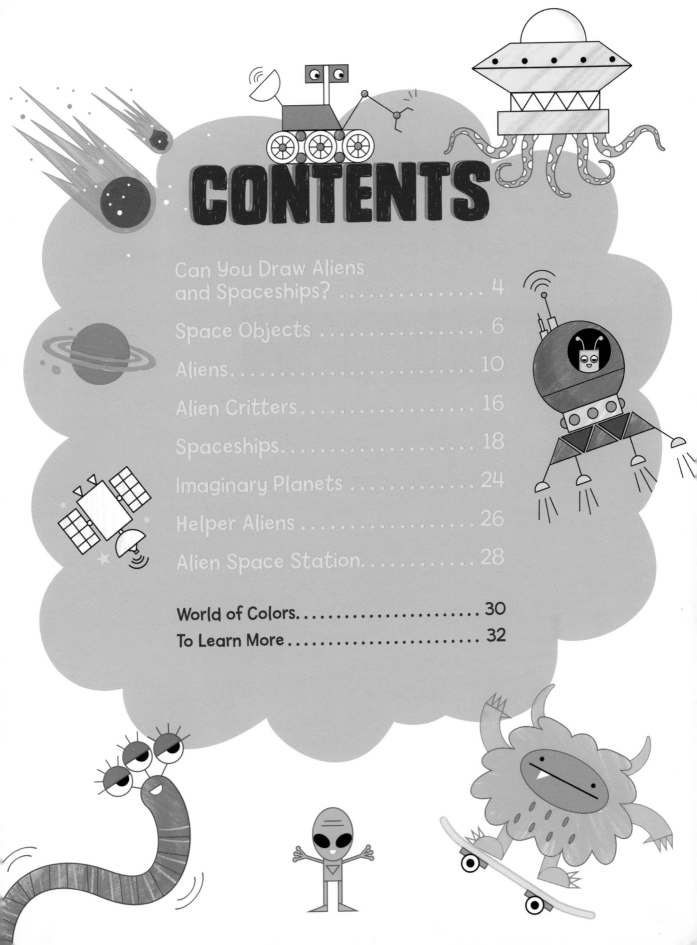

CONTENTS

CAN YOU DRAW ALIENS AND SPACESHIPS?

You can if you can draw shapes! Use the shapes in the box at the top of each page to draw the alien or spaceship parts. Put the parts together in your drawing to make an awesome alien or a zooming rocket. Or, use the parts to make your own alien or spaceship!

ALIEN AND SPACESHIP PARTS

Shapes you will use: circle   trapezoid   rectangle   half circle   square   triangle

Eyes

Tentacles

Hands

Mouths

 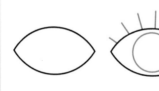 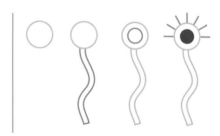

Rocket Boosters

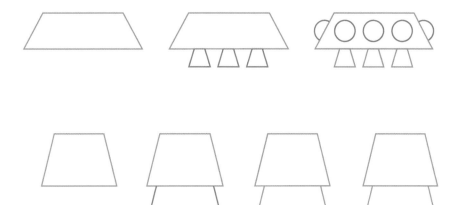

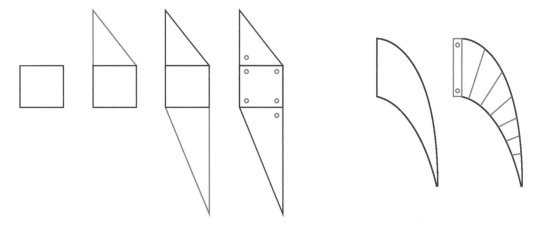

Wings

Wheels

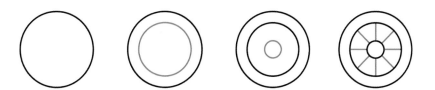

SPACE OBJECTS

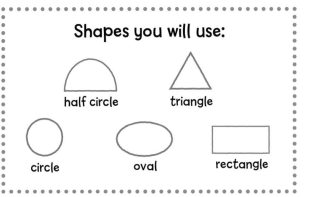

Sun

Moon

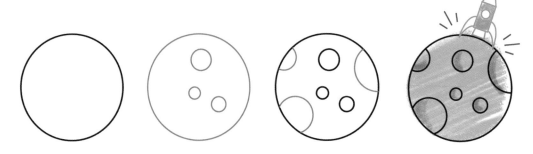

Jupiter

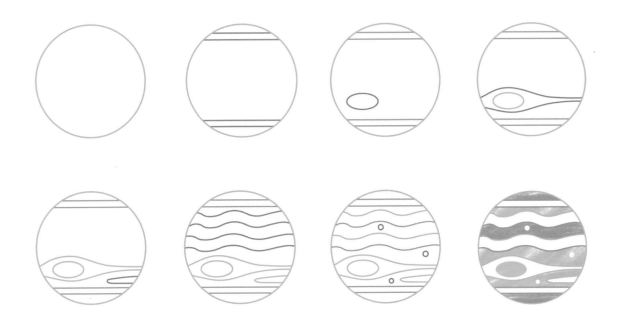

Shooting Star

circle   triangle   rectangle

Saturn

Comet

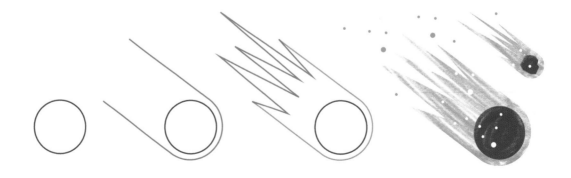

Galaxy

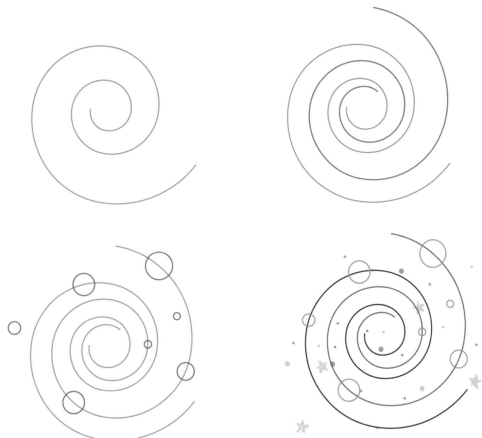

Telescope

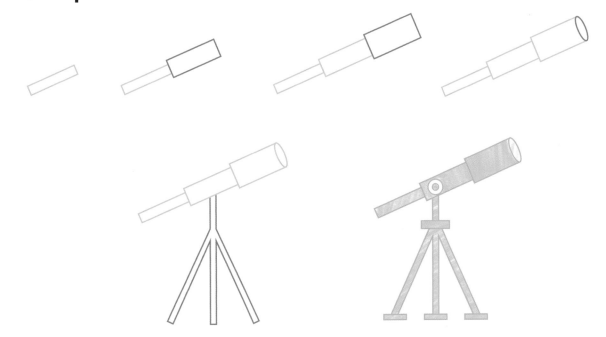

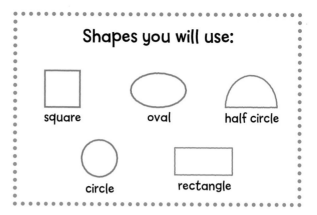

Shapes you will use:

square   oval   half circle

circle   rectangle

Roly-Poly

Frank

Rockin' Alien

Bugsy

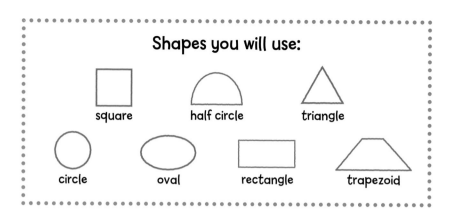

Shapes you will use:

square half circle triangle

circle oval rectangle trapezoid

Boogie

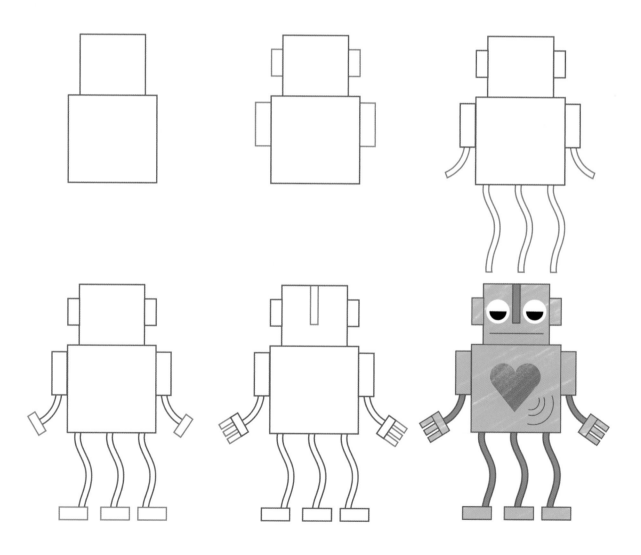

Little Green Man

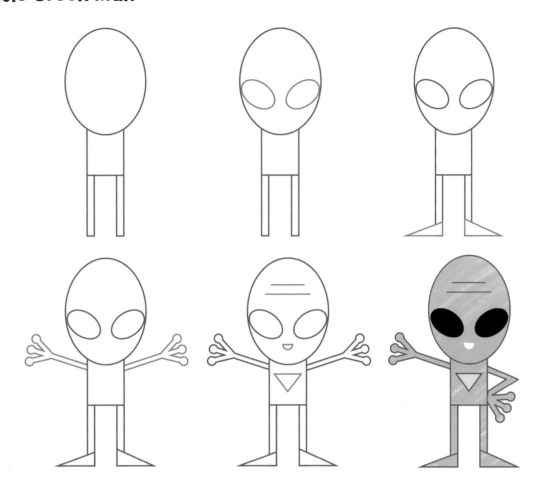

Hovering Alien

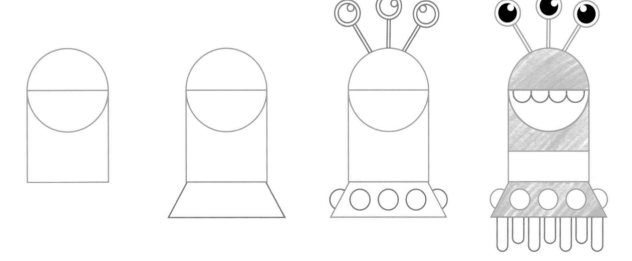

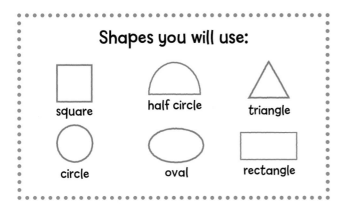
Jammer

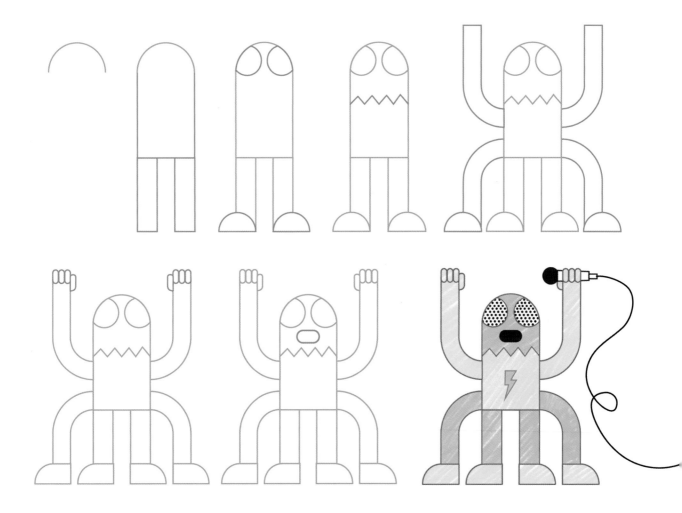

Hairy

Cyclops

15

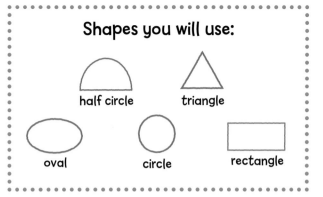
Space Worm

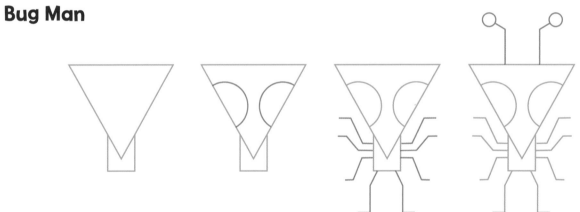

Bug Man

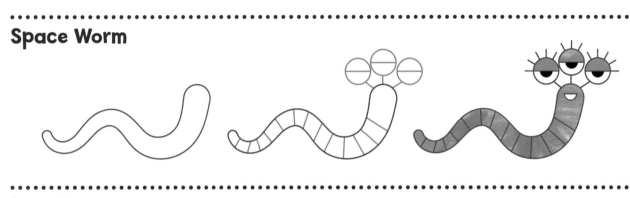

Space Spider

Three Eyes

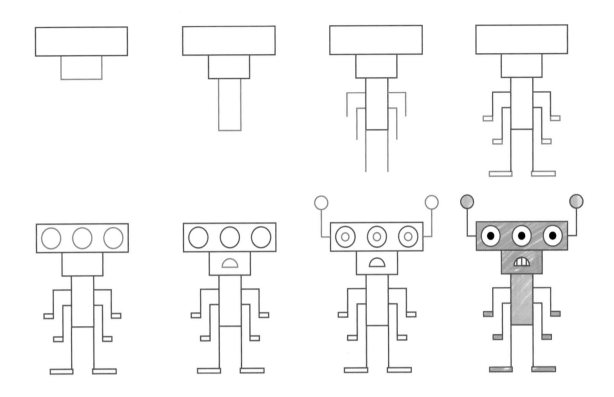

Buzz

17

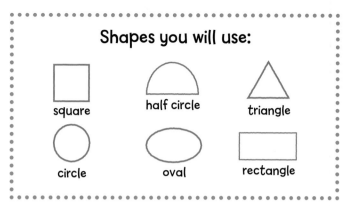
Flying Saucer

Blaster

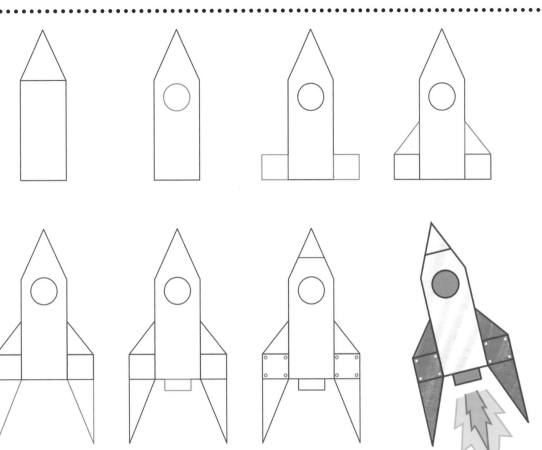

Satellite

19

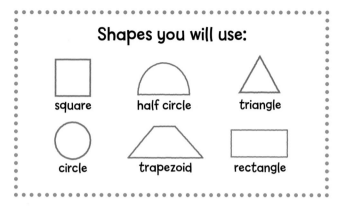

Shapes you will use:

square · half circle · triangle · circle · trapezoid · rectangle

Rocket Racer

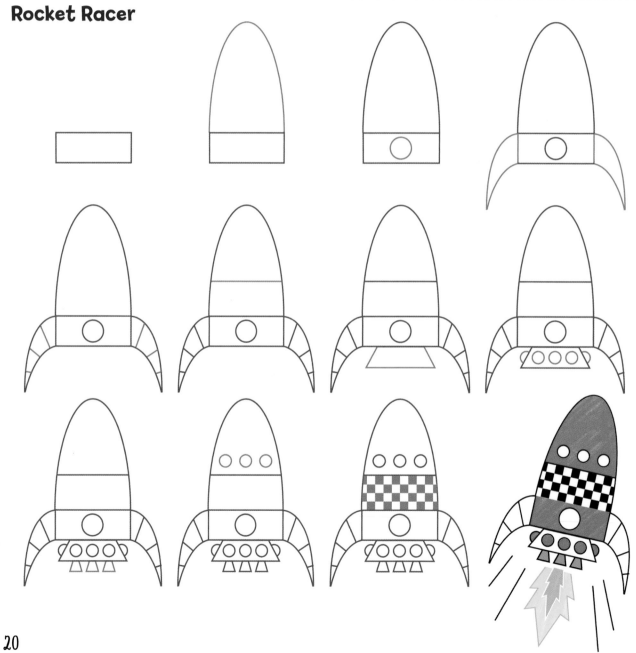

Rover

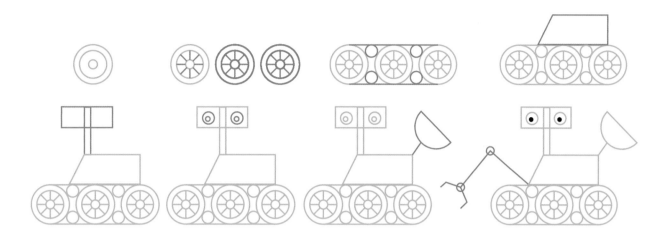

Jet Speeder

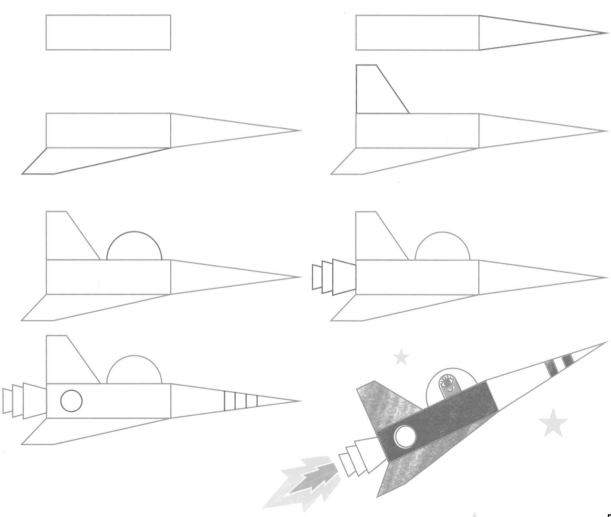

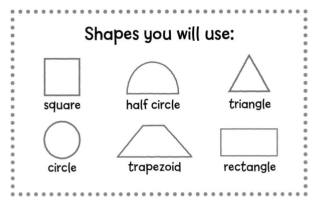

Shapes you will use:

square   half circle   triangle

circle   trapezoid   rectangle

Bubble Pod

Tentacle Ship

Starfighter

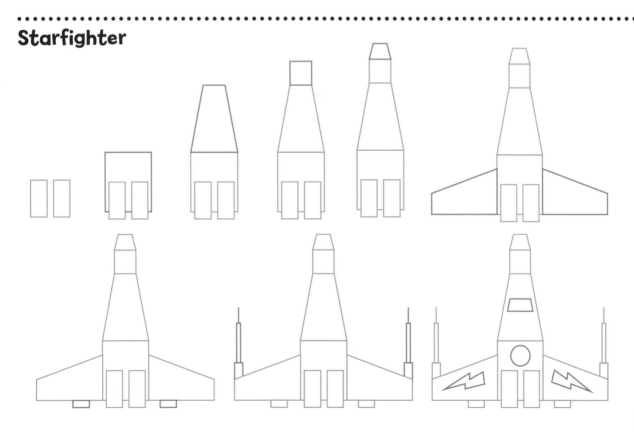

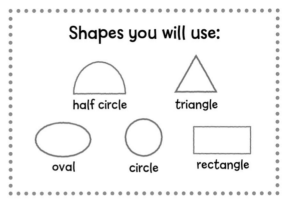
Planet Burgertron!

Magical Planet

HELPER ALIENS

Doctor Alien

Traffic Cop Alien

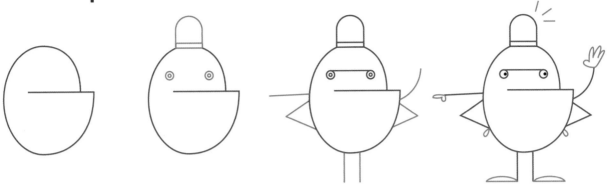

Firefighter Alien

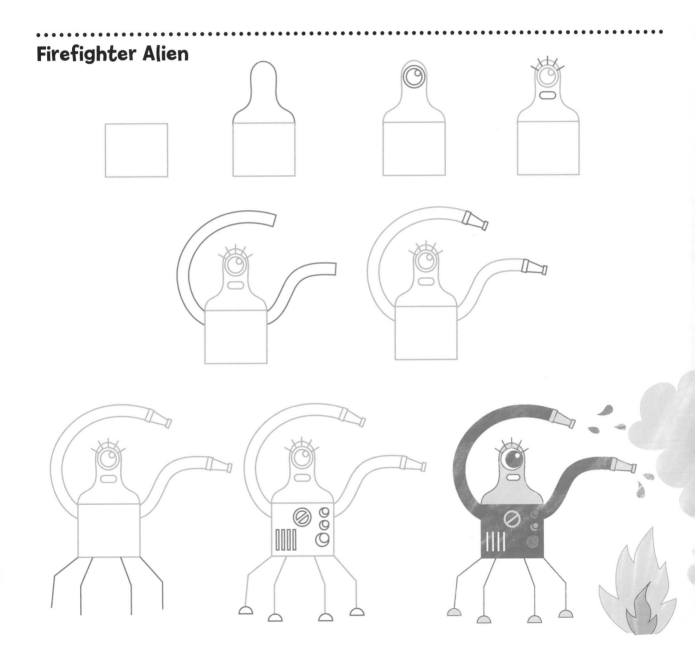

SPACE SNACKS

28

ALIEN SPACE STATION

WORLD OF COLORS

The universe is full of colors! Here are some of the Crayola® crayon colors used in this book. What colors will you use to draw your next outer space adventure?

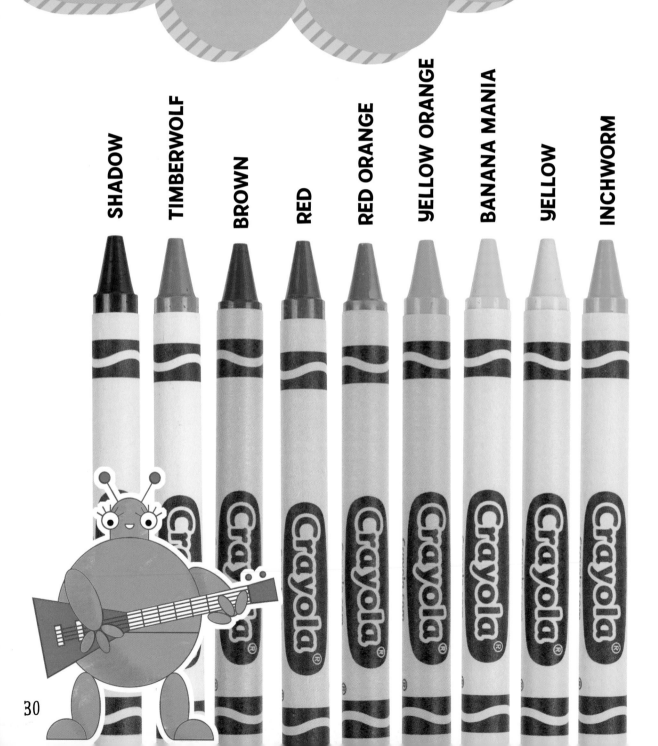

SHADOW **TIMBERWOLF** **BROWN** **RED** **RED ORANGE** **YELLOW ORANGE** **BANANA MANIA** **YELLOW** **INCHWORM**

THERE'S ALWAYS SPACE TO DRAW!

YELLOW GREEN

SKY BLUE

NAVY BLUE

OUTER SPACE

VIVID VIOLET

ORCHID

MAGENTA

PINK FLAMINGO

PINK SHERBERT

TO LEARN MORE

Books

Bergin, Mark. *It's Fun to Draw Robots and Aliens*. New York: Sky Pony Press, 2014. Get more practice drawing your favorite robots and aliens with this book.

Garbot, Dave. *Space Aliens*. Lake Forest, CA: Walter Foster Publishing, 2016. Check out this book to learn how to draw some hilarious aliens.

Let's Draw Robots with Crayola! Illustrated by Emily Golden. Minneapolis: Lerner Publications, 2018. Take a look at this book if you like drawing robots just as much as you like drawing aliens!

Websites

Alien Puppet
http://www.crayola.com/crafts/alien-puppet-craft/
Visit this website to learn how to turn your favorite alien drawing into a puppet.

Learn to Draw Space Pictures
https://www.activityvillage.co.uk/learn-to-draw-space-pictures
Draw even more aliens, spaceships, and more with this website.